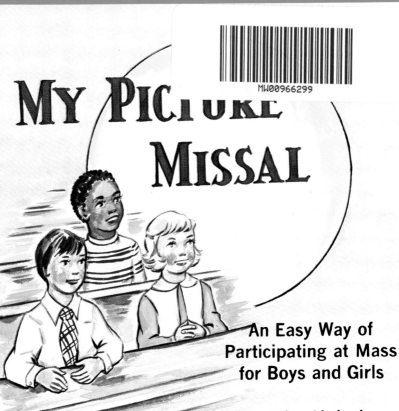

MY PICTURE MISSAL

An Easy Way of
Participating at Mass
for Boys and Girls

The words said aloud
are in heavy black print.

By REV. LAWRENCE G. LOVASIK, S.V.D.
Divine Word Missionary

NIHIL OBSTAT: Daniel V. Flynn, J.C.D., *Censor Librorum*
IMPRIMATUR: ✠ James P. Mahoney, D.D., *Vicar General, Archdiocese of New York*

© 1978 by *Catholic Book Publishing Corp.*, N.J. — Printed in Hong Kong   ISBN 978-0-89942-275-6

THE ORDER OF MASS

We begin our celebration of the Eucharist

We sing the Entrance Song and then make the
sign of the cross.   <u>STAND</u>

I N THE name of the Father, and of the Son,
and of the Holy Spirit.

PEOPLE: Amen.

English translations © 1969 International Committee on English in the Liturgy, Inc.
Other texts and illustrations © 1979 Copyright by Catholic Book Publishing Corp., N.J.

THE GREETING

PRIEST: The grace of our Lord Jesus Christ and the love of God and the fellowship of the Holy Spirit be with you all.

PEOPLE: And also with you.

OR ─────────────────────────────

PRIEST: The grace and peace of God our Father and the Lord Jesus Christ be with you.

PEOPLE: Blessed be God, the Father and our Lord Jesus Christ.

OR ─────────────────────────────

PEOPLE: And also with you.

OR ─────────────────────────────

PRIEST: The Lord be with you.

PEOPLE: And also with you.

3

THE PENITENTIAL RITE

Jesus loves us and forgives all our sins as long as we are really sorry for them.

I CONFESS to almighty God
and to you, my brothers and sisters,
that I have sinned through my own fault

They strike their breast:

**in my thoughts and in my words,
in what I have done,
and in what I have failed to do;
and I ask blessed Mary, ever virgin,
all the angels and saints,
and you, my brothers and sisters,
to pray for me to the Lord our God.**

PRIEST:

May almighty God have mercy on us, forgive us our sins, and bring us to ever-lasting life.

PEOPLE: **Amen.**

We ask Jesus for mercy

THE KYRIE

PRIEST: Lord, have mercy.
PEOPLE: **Lord, have mercy.**

PRIEST: Christ, have mercy.
PEOPLE: **Christ, have mercy.**

PRIEST: Lord, have mercy.
PEOPLE: **Lord, have mercy.**

THE GLORIA

PEOPLE:

GLORY to God in the highest,
and peace to his people on earth.
Lord God, heavenly King,
almighty God and Father,
    we worship you, we give you thanks,
    we praise you for your glory.
Lord Jesus Christ, only Son of the Father,
Lord God, Lamb of God,
you take away the sin of the world:
    have mercy on us;
you are seated at the right hand of the Father:
    receive our prayer.

For you alone are the Holy One,
you alone are the Lord,
you alone are the Most High,
    Jesus Christ,
    with the Holy Spirit,
    in the glory of God the Father.
        Amen.

We pray for all our needs

THE OPENING PRAYER

O LORD, help us to love you so that we may imitate you.

We ask you this through our Lord Jesus Christ, your Son, who lives and reigns with you and the Holy Spirit, one God, for ever and ever. **PEOPLE: Amen.**

God speaks to us

By means of readings taken from the Holy **Bible**, God speaks to us through his prophets and apostles. Most of all, he speaks to us through his **Son Jesus.** Jesus is as present to us as he was to the people of Palestine.

God speaks to us through the Prophets

THE FIRST READING   SIT

We sit and listen to the word of God.

At the end of the reading:

READER: The word of the Lord.

PEOPLE: **Thanks be to God.**

We respond to God's Word

RESPONSORIAL PSALM

The people repeat the response

God speaks to us through the Apostles

THE SECOND READING

At the end:

READER: The word of the Lord.

PEOPLE: **Thanks be to God.**

THE GOSPEL

We stand up to listen while the priest proclaims the Gospel in the name of Jesus. Jesus himself becomes present among us through his Word.

STAND

The Priest speaks

PRIEST: The Lord be with you.

PEOPLE: And also with you.

DEACON (or priest):
A reading from the holy gospel according to N.

PEOPLE: Glory to you, Lord.

We listen to the Priest read the Word of God.

At the end:

The Gospel of the Lord.

PEOPLE: Praise to you, Lord Jesus Christ.

God speaks to us through the Priest

THE HOMILY

The homily helps us to put the words of Christ into practice.

PROFESSION OF FAITH—THE APOSTLES' CREED

I BELIEVE in God, the Father almighty,   STAND
        creator of heaven and earth.

I BELIEVE in Jesus Christ, his only Son, our Lord.
    He was conceived by the power of the Holy
        Spirit
    and born of the Virgin Mary.
    He suffered under Pontius Pilate,
        was crucified, died, and was buried.
    He descended to the dead.
    On the third day he rose again.
    He ascended into heaven,
        and is seated at the right hand of the
            Father.
    He will come again to judge the living and
        the dead.

I believe in the Holy Spirit,
    the holy catholic Church,
    the communion of saints,
    the forgiveness of sins,
    the resurrection of the body,
    and the life everlasting. Amen.

─────────── OR — THE NICENE CREED ───────────

WE BELIEVE in one God,
        the Father, the Almighty,
    maker of heaven and earth,
    of all that is seen and unseen.

12

We believe in one Lord, JESUS CHRIST,
the only Son of God,
eternally begotten of the Father,
God from God, Light from Light,
true God from true God,
begotten, not made, one in Being with the Father

Through him all things were made.
For us men and for our salvation
he came down from heaven:
All bow at the following words up to: and became man.

by the power of the Holy Spirit
he was born of the Virgin Mary, and became man.

For our sake he was crucified under Pontius Pilate;
he suffered, died, and was buried.
On the third day he rose again
in fulfillment of the Scriptures;
he ascended into heaven
and is seated at the right hand of the Father.

He will come again in glory to judge
the living and the dead,
and his kingdom will have no end.

We believe in the HOLY SPIRIT,
the Lord, the giver of life,
who proceeds from the Father and the Son.

With the Father and the Son he is worshiped and glorified.

He has spoken through the Prophets.

We believe in one holy catholic and apostolic Church.

We acknowledge one baptism for the forgiveness of sins.

We look for the resurrection of the dead,
and the life of the world to come. Amen.

GENERAL INTERCESSIONS

(Prayer of the Faithful)

After the priest gives the introduction, the deacon or other minister sings or says the invocations.

PEOPLE: **Lord, hear our prayer.**

(or other response, according to local custom)

At the end the priest says the concluding prayer.

PEOPLE: **Amen.**

THE LITURGY OF THE EUCHARIST

PREPARATION OF THE ALTAR AND THE GIFTS

SIT

While the gifts of the people are brought forward to the priest and are placed on the altar, the offertory song may be sung.

15

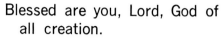

We offer bread

PREPARATION OF THE BREAD

Blessed are you, Lord, God of
  all creation.
Through your goodness we have
  this bread to offer,
which earth has given and
  human hands have made.
It will become for us the bread
  of life.

PEOPLE:

Blessed be God for ever.

We offer wine

PREPARATION OF THE WINE

Blessed are you, Lord, God of
  all creation.
Through your goodness we have
  this wine to offer,
fruit of the vine and work of
  human hands.
It will become our spiritual
  drink.

PEOPLE:

Blessed be God for ever.

INVITATION TO PRAYER   <u>STAND</u>

PRIEST: Pray, brethren, that our sacrifice may be acceptable to God, the almighty Father.

PEOPLE: **May the Lord accept the sacrifice at your hands**
for the praise and glory of his name,
for our good, and the good of all his Church.

PRAYER OVER THE GIFTS

LORD God,
through your sacraments
you give us the power of your grace.
May this Eucharist
help us to serve you faithfully.
We ask this in the name of Jesus the Lord.

PEOPLE: **Amen.**

EUCHARISTIC PRAYER

PRIEST: The Lord be with you.
PEOPLE: **And also with you.**

PRIEST: Lift up your hearts.
PEOPLE: **We lift them up to the Lord.**

PRIEST: Let us give thanks to the Lord our God.
PEOPLE: **It is right to give him thanks and praise.**

We praise You for this sacrifice

THE PREFACE

We listen to the priest read the Preface.

We praise God in union with the angels

PEOPLE:

HOLY, HOLY, HOLY Lord,
God of power and might,
heaven and earth are full of your glory.
Hosanna in the highest.
Blessed is he who comes in the name of the Lord.
Hosanna in the highest.

KNEEL

19

At Mass Jesus offers himself again

DEAR Father in heaven,
      in great pain
Jesus gave himself to you
upon the Cross
and begged you to forgive us.

Jesus now gives himself to you
in this Holy Mass
but he does not suffer anymore.

Prayer for the Holy Spirit

LORD,
we pray that the Holy Spirit
may come upon these gifts
and make them holy.

May they become for us
the body and blood
of Our Lord Jesus Christ.

Jesus at the Last Supper — The First Mass

CONSECRATION OF THE BREAD

AT THE Last Supper, on the day before Jesus died on the cross, he took bread into his holy hands.

He raised his eyes to you, O God, his almighty Father, and gave thanks to you.

He blessed it, broke it and gave it to his disciples, saying:

Take this, all of you, and eat it:

this is my body which will be given

up for you.

ELEVATION OF THE HOST

After changing the bread into the living body of Jesus, the priest shows the consecrated Bread to the people, places it on the paten, and genuflects in adoration.

Adore the Sacred Host and say:

"My Lord and my God!"

CONSECRATION OF THE WINE

The priest changes the wine into the living Blood of Jesus. He uses the same words Jesus used at the Last Supper.

TAKE this, all of you, and drink from it:
this is the cup of my blood,
the blood of the new and everlasting covenant.
It will be shed for you and for all
so that sins may be forgiven.
Do this in memory of me.

We proclaim the Mystery of our faith

MEMORIAL ACCLAMATION

We now acclaim Our Lord Jesus Christ who is with us on the altar. We remember his Passion, Death, and Resurrection and his Return on the Last Day.

PRIEST: Let us proclaim the mystery of faith.

PEOPLE:

A Christ has died,
Christ is risen,
Christ will come again.

———————— OR ————————

B Dying you destroyed our death,
rising you restored our life,
Lord Jesus, come in glory.

———————— OR ————————

C When we eat this bread and drink this cup,
we proclaim your death, Lord Jesus,
until you come in glory.

———————— OR ————————

D Lord, by your cross and resurrection
you have set us free.
You are the Savior of the world.

THE GREAT AMEN

We give our assent to all that has taken place

PRIEST:

Through him, with him, in him, in the unity of the Holy Spirit, all glory and honor is yours, almighty Father, for ever and ever.

At the end of the Eucharistic Prayer, we join the priest in giving glory to the Father through Jesus by saying or singing the Great Amen.

PEOPLE: **Amen.**

COMMUNION RITE   **STAND**

THE LORD'S PRAYER

PRIEST: Let us pray with confidence to the Father in the words our Savior gave us:

PRIEST and PEOPLE:

**OUR FATHER, who art in heaven,
hallowed be thy name;
thy kingdom come;
thy will be done on earth as it is in heaven.
Give us this day our daily bread;
and forgive us our trespasses
as we forgive those who trespass against us;
and lead us not into temptation,
but deliver us from evil.**

PRIEST: Deliver us, Lord, from every evil, and grant us peace in our day. In your mercy keep us free from sin and protect us from all anxiety as we wait in joyful hope for the coming of our Savior, Jesus Christ.

PEOPLE: **For the kingdom, the power, and the glory are yours, now and for ever.**

SIGN OF PEACE

PRIEST: For ever and ever.

PEOPLE: Amen.

PRIEST: The peace of the Lord be with you always.

PEOPLE: And also with you.

PRIEST: Let us offer each other the sign of peace.

PEOPLE: BREAKING OF THE BREAD

LAMB of God, you take away the sins of the world:
   have mercy on us.

Lamb of God, you take away the sins of the world:
   have mercy on us.

Lamb of God, you take away the sins of the world:
   grant us peace.

<u>**KNEEL**</u>

PRIEST: This is the Lamb of God
   who takes away the sins of the world.
   Happy are those who are called to his supper.

PRIEST and **PEOPLE:**

**Lord, I am not worthy
to receive you,
but only say the word
and I shall be healed.**

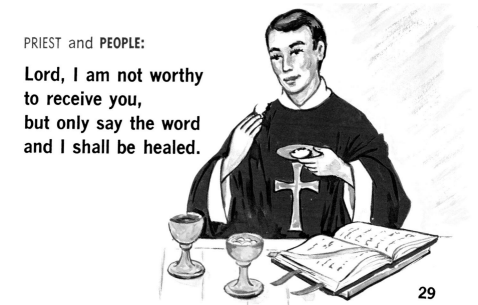

We receive Jesus in Holy Communion

A Communion Song may be sung while communion is given to the faithful.

The Priest then gives communion to the people.

PRIEST: The body of Christ.   PEOPLE: Amen.

A private prayer after Communion:

Jesus, I believe that you have come to me
in Holy Communion.   SIT
I hope in you because you are all-good
I love you with all my heart,
because you deserve all my love.

PRAYER AFTER COMMUNION

PRIEST: Through Christ our Lord.   <u>STAND</u>
PEOPLE: **Amen.**

CONCLUDING RITE

PRIEST: The Lord be with you.
PEOPLE: **And also with you.**

We receive God's blessing from the priest

THE BLESSING

PRIEST: May almighty God bless you, the Father, and the Son, ✠ and the Holy Spirit.
PEOPLE: **Amen.**

God sends us out to bring Christ to others

DISMISSAL

DEACON (or priest):

A Go in the peace of Christ.
——————————— **OR** ———————————
B The Mass is ended, go in peace.
——————————— **OR** ———————————
C Go in peace to love and serve the Lord.

PEOPLE: Thanks be to God.

The priest dismisses us and we go home to live as good Christians.